Live Right to Live Well

THE TRUTH ABOUT PROSPEROUS LIVING

DR. A. WAYNE COOK

authorHOUSE®

AuthorHouse™
1663 Liberty Drive
Bloomington, IN 47403
www.authorhouse.com
Phone: 1 (800) 839-8640

Published by AuthorHouse 03/28/2018

ISBN: 978-1-5462-3387-9 (sc)
ISBN: 978-1-5462-3386-2 (e)

Print information available on the last page.

PREFACE

"Pastor, I know God is going to help me win the lottery...I'm going to give my tithe to the church and you will be able to build that new building with the money." That is the attitude many people have about money and prosperity. That reflects their belief that prosperity is about how much money a person has. The most telling part of this statement is the concept that if we simply have faith in Christ, He will bless our lives with more money and material things.

Many people have a rabid appetite to live well. Prosperity is the "American Dream." Many preachers and pastors, especially those in mega churches and on television preach a "Prosperity Theology." Their premise is simple: have a relationship with God and everything will turn out right and He will work miracles and rain down blessings and you will live a rich man's lifestyle and have the best of everything. God will give health and wealth like you have never had before. (The next thing out of their mouth is, "Just send your seed offering to us and God will multiply it ten-fold.") But they forget some of the principles of how to live well. One should live right in order to live well.

It would seem no one would prefer to live wrong. Nobody tries to deliberately live in such a way as to harm other people or cause their own lives to be ruined. There are some who make choices to live that way, and they pay the price and pay dearly.

Books by the thousands are sold each year dealing with how to succeed or how to accomplish great things. But not many books start with the premise of instructing people how to live *right.*

America and probably the whole world is obsessed with living well. Go to the local big box stores and you will have an idea how much the average person desires to live well and own the latest toys and gadgets.

A new ad campaign on television for investing in precious metals ends with the slogan, "Live Well." Just invest in these metals instead of other investments and you will be rolling in riches.

My conviction is that it is more important to live right than to live well. In fact, living right should result in living well. Read Psalm 1 and you will see God's way of blessing those who live right. It is contrary to society's formula of hard work, believing in one's self and having a positive attitude. It is a statement of the life that God blesses so that one can live well.

Part of the problem is that even churches and preachers have fallen into the mistaken philosophy of "prosperity theology." That is, "If God loves you, He must send His blessing in the form of monetary prosperity to show that love." They are false teachers, leading many people astray with promises of financial prosperity without teaching them they must be saved by the blood of Christ through repentance and faith. After one comes to Christ, the believer's life involves following the principles of obedience and living right and allowing God to bless them with His presence and the reward of the prosperous life. In order to understand His perspective regarding prosperity, it is necessary for one to understand some basic facts.

God does not think like man. He does not equate love with money and material things. Jesus showed us the greatest love known to man. He talked more about money than He did about Heaven. But He never said, "Follow me and I will make you prosperous financially."

This book is part of that small group of titles and manuscripts intended for helping others to *live right*. It should also help one to *live well*. That is in contrast to the modern "prosperity theology" that says, "Follow Jesus, and He will bless you by giving you all you ever desired, especially materially and financially." That is in deep conflict with what Jesus Himself offered during His earthly ministry. He offered a life of poverty, sacrifice, and often conflict.

Understand that I have dealt with people in my ministry many years and observed them from various angles. I have seen them in stress, in recreation, as sports fans, in competition, in grief and sorrow, and every family situation you can imagine. Most people have a strong desire to live right. I have witnessed victory, prosperity, poverty, and leadership.

People want to live right! People want to live well.

First, they want to live right in order to insure their standing and their future in society. People living with wrong character, wrong attitudes, and wrong lifestyles, are shunned or discriminated against by various elements of our society. They often cut their own lives short. Many of them end up in poverty, incarceration, or ruin.

Those who live right are not only accepted in society, but are kept in high regard. They are respected and sought out for honor and wisdom. They are the ones who earn awards and promotions in the workplace.

Secondly, they want to live right in order to protect their legacies. Most people are aware of what they are leaving behind for the family. It most often takes the form of financial or material estates. They also leave behind a sense of well-being. Family trees become vital in the lives of the next generation. Living well will leave an estate; living right will help one to live well. Those who get the principles reversed will have negative results.

One of the saddest things to watch, is the multi-millionaire athletes who use their platform to influence younger people to follow in their footsteps of greed, anger, and mistreatment of others. Many of them are abusers of their mates, or they become angry people in our society.

Some of them say, "I don't want to become an example to the youth of our city and nation." But they cannot avoid that position. Stardom comes with fame and a following. Certainly in that setting, "No man is an island. No one can live unto themselves."

Someone has said, "The fact that people are watching motivates me to keep my life clean." That is a strong statement worth living for.

Facebook posts can be informative as to how people think. One post recently featured the name of about a dozen famous football players and listed how many children they had by a number of different mothers. Several of them had 6 children by 5 women for example. The influence on the next generation will negate the fame and fortune earned on the field.

There have been some really fine athletic stars who are leaving strong positive legacies for their children and those youngsters who look up to their athletic heroes. Such legacies far surpass the money they leave behind.

Finally, people want to live right because it affects their standing in eternity, the afterlife. Some believe the way they live determines their eternal destination. Those who believe that eternity rests in the hands of a God who offers grace and mercy when it comes to justice and judgment and being assured of Heaven by accepting Christ as Savior, at least have in their belief system a value of how good they will have it in Heaven if they live right on earth. (I stand with the latter belief.)

In this book, I have attempted to show some principles from God's word that He promises will produce prosperity in one's life. Take these principles and apply them to your thinking and watch how often you will make right choices and right decisions. If you do, you will live right.

It should be noted at this point that prosperity is not something that occurs instantaneously when a person decides to follow Christ. It is something that happens as a result of a lifetime (or at least several years) of following God's instructions for the prosperous life.

Let's consider God's instructions.

DISCUSSION QUESTIONS

1. Which reason do you think that most people would give for living well?
2. Can you think of any other reasons people might wish to live well?
3. Read Isaiah 55:8-9 and discuss or think about how many ways God's ways are higher than our ways.

CHAPTER ONE

LIVE WITH A STRONG SENSE OF RIGHT AND WRONG

Someone was quoted recently that I overheard. It was said, "live so that people will want your autograph, not your fingerprints." I find that to be good advice. It comes from living right

The Bible says, "There is a way that seems right to a man, But its end is the way of death." (Proverbs 14:12 NKJV) There is a necessity of knowing exactly what is right or wrong. How can a person make the right choices and make good decisions without such knowledge.

It is impossible to live your life right if you do not know what is right and what is wrong. It is amazing that as people have increased knowledge and obtained more information, they have lost the ability to discern what is right and wrong.

In fact, society in general has now established a different measure of deciding if actions and thinking are right. Some think that if a great majority of people accept it, then it must be right. But even that does not work well, because a couple years later (or sooner) the majority of people may reject it for one reason or another.

It started with "situation ethics", a term to mean what is right in one situation becomes wrong in another situation. People then tend to decide something is wrong if it is causing them to act differently or if the circumstances causes pain. The reasoning is that it becomes wrong if failure or incompleteness is the result. In other words, it becomes right if things turn out right for the person doing it.

Sometimes, doing right causes pain or discomfort. It is more important to do right than to end up winning or feeling good. Why else would people respect martyrs, people who die for a cause?

This standard of thinking and doing often causes one to lose sight of truth. In reality, truth should never change. If truth changes with the situation then there is no absolute.

I know that may be considered overly simplified reasoning but if truth changes, one can no longer discern what is good or bad, right or wrong, or winning or losing. Usually, the result of such reasoning ends up being circular thinking, returning to a lack of conclusion regarding living right.

The sadness is, the situation ethics concept has led to every person deciding his/her own right and wrong. Ultimately, one ends up expecting people to respect one's conclusion but refusing to honor someone else's conclusion. Therefore, anarchy becomes the reality of society's existence. It happened in the Old Testament. "Every man did that which was right in his own eyes." (Judges 21:25)

Proverbs 21:2 speaks about such behavior. "Every way of a man is right in his own eyes: but the Lord pondereth the hearts."(KJV) People consider their own ways to be right, regardless of what others think and what God thinks.

As I said, Proverbs 14:12 points out the danger of such thinking. It says "There is a way that seems right to a man, But its end is the way of death." (NKJV) Man's thought processes try to work through circumstances by common sense or by whatever ways they try to make decisions. That can cause an assumption that a certain decision is right, but be fatally wrong. That is what causes the problem with situation ethics. It depends too much on man's flawed thinking and reasoning. After all, the human heart is desperately wicked according to God's word.

When our children were growing up, we tried to instill in them and live in front of them with the philosophy that was promoted by University President and Evangelist, Dr. Bob Jones, Sr. He said, "Do right, even if the stars fall. Do right."

My wife sat under his tutelage for over three years. She also had a Pastor at her home church who kept hammering away at the same philosophy nearly every Sunday. Though it was not stated just this way, my parents, church, and school instilled the same philosophy into my psyche.

Public opinion will change depending on the cultural and social emphases of the day. Right will always be right.

Our children have repeatedly as children, teens, and now as adults with their own families been put to the test. Their desire to do right has molded their character and people's opinions of them have come as a result of that unwavering character.

Our son is an attorney. He graduated from law school at the age of 50 (one month before his 51st birthday) and passed the bar exam on his first attempt. He then started his own practice. People are coming to him and have promised when they need an attorney's services, he will be the one they seek. The reason they give is that they know his integrity. Others around Central Virginia are taking note of his honesty and integrity as well.

Two of our daughters are involved with providing childcare for preschoolers. They are both in high demand privately and can just about name their hours and prices for private care. Parents in the centers where they work go to them about how to raise their children with integrity and character. Their love for children also shows constantly.

Our other daughter works in another field entirely but she too is noted by the organization in which she works for her integrity. The leaders know that she will tell the truth and will not cut corners in the processes and systems.

One company's employee was put in a difficult situation where there were conflicting stories. One manager told another they knew the truth because the employee said it. His character and integrity spoke for itself.

How does one know when they are telling the truth and how can they determine what is right or wrong?

It really is quite simple. Tell what exactly happened or what exactly exists, not what one's opinion of it is, or how one wishes it to be. Truth cannot be set or determined by anyone's "take" on it. We cannot use or look for ulterior motives or underlying intentions by others or ourselves. The old adage -- "It is what it is," certainly applies here.

Rick Warren wrote a devotional about truth:

> "**Change Requires Learning The Truth**
>
> *You will never change the things in your life that you know are defective unless you learn the truth. Change*

requires learning the truth. You're not going to be free until you know the truth. The secret to personal change is not a pill, program, or process. It's not therapy, a book, or a seminar. It's not positive thinking or psychology. The proof of personal change is found in the truth. You have to know and face the truth about yourself, God, and your relationships before you can change.

"Behind every self-defeating behavior in your life is a lie you're believing. If you're deeply in debt right now, it's because you believed some lies. You thought, "I can just keep charging it forever and get away with it." Oh really? "I have to have this house." Oh really? Do you really have to have it? Is it true? Can you prove it? We lie to ourselves all the time. But you have to know and face the truth if you're going to change.

Jesus said the truth will set you free. But first it makes you miserable! It makes you miserable as long as you deny it. The moment that you are honest with the truth about you and everything else in life, then it starts to set you free.

Who is the truth? Jesus said, "I am the truth." Not "I have it." Not "I point the way." Not "I teach it." He said, "I'm it. I am the truth."

You can trust his Word. His Word is the Bible.

The Bible is good for four things: "All Scripture is God-breathed and is useful for teaching, rebuking, correcting and training in righteousness, so that the servant of God may be thoroughly equipped for every good work" (2 Timothy 3:16-17 NIV).

The Bible is like a path. It shows us where to walk and how to stay on the path. It shows us when we get off the path and how to get back on the path. When you use God's Word *to show you where and how you should walk, it will give you the instruction and knowledge you need to change your life."*

In order to determine what is right or wrong, there needs to be a measuring stick of truth, an unswerving measurement. I have only found one measurement that is eternally and unequivocally true and right. There is one book that has proven to be that measurement above all other. *It is the Bible.* One must allow right and wrong to be determined by that unwavering measurement.

How can a person to be sure to walk in that rightness? Let's consider a few guidelines to make that happen.

1. Trust the Bible as God's written word to man. As I accept the Bible as God's direct word to me, I can then accept it as that which determines whether any idea, thought, motive or action is right. If it disagrees with the Bible, then it is wrong.

In the Old Testament, God gave The Law. It is found in the writings presented by Moses in the Pentateuch. God gave Moses those laws directly, face to face, on Mount Sinai. They are codified in The Ten Commandments, which most of man's laws and courts are copied after or at least they are influenced by them. When Jesus was asked by the lawyers of His day what the greatest commandment was (trying to trick him, by the way), He said, "...You shall love the Lord your God with all your heart, with all your soul, and with all your mind. This is the first and great commandment." Not stopping with that, he said, "And the second is like it. You shall love your neighbor as yourself." (Matthew 22:37-39 NKJV)

2. Commit your life, soul, and mind to the Lord Jesus Christ. This is so important. Without Jesus in your life, it is destined to be a wrongly lived life. In fact, it is not life at all, but death. John 3:36 says, "He that hath the Son hath life, but he that hath not the Son of God hath not life, but the wrath of God abideth on Him." (KJV)

The whole reason of Jesus dying on the cross and rising from the dead was to give eternal, everlasting life to those who receive Him into their lives and commit their lives to Him.

A person can do this in a simple manner. Repent of the sinful condition where all people live ("All have sinned and come short of the glory of God." Romans 3:23 KJV), turn to Christ and call upon His name, asking Him to forgive the sin in your life and accept you as one of His followers.

This is what Christians are talking about when we say, "being saved." It is the way to be "born again." It secures a place in Heaven and brings forgiveness, giving a new life to the one who believes and calls on the name of Jesus Christ.

The Apostle, John, summed it up well: "He that hath the Son hath life; and he that hath not the Son of God hath not life." (I John 5:12 KJV)

3. Receive the Holy Spirit's Power. This is a further action that takes place when one receives the Son of God into our lives: The Holy Spirit then lives in us as our guide and empowering force. When someone receives salvation through Jesus, He sends the Holy Spirit to live in the heart, soul, and spirit of the believer.

Jesus made a wonderful statement In Acts 1:8 in a conversation with the disciples after His resurrection. He instructed them to return into Jerusalem and wait for the coming of the Holy Spirit. His promise was, "You shall

RECEIVE POWER after that the Holy Spirit comes upon you and you shall become witnesses unto me in Jerusalem, Judea, Samaria and unto the uttermost parts of the earth." (Acts 1:8 KJV, Caps mine)

4. Walk in the Spirit. The Apostle Paul wrote a letter to the church in Galatia. In it, he described the battle that goes on inside all of us between the evils of sin in the flesh (self desires). He described the works of the flesh in Galatians 5:19-21:

Adultery
Fornication
Uncleanness
Lasciviousness (Evil-doing)
Idolatry
Witchcraft
Hatred
Variance (Inconsistency or wavering from righteousness)
Emulations (Jealousy)
Wrath
Strife
Seditions
Heresies
Envyings
Murders
Drunkenness
Revellings (Partying)
And such like.

Quite the list isn't it? It is not a list of character and personality traits that we look for in an ideal person, is it?

Then he describes the fruit that comes from the Spirit of God within the believer:

Love
Joy,
Peace,
Longsuffering (Patience)
Gentleness
Goodness
Faith
Meekness
Temperance,
(Galatians 5:22 KJV)

At the end of that same chapter in Galatians, Paul said, "Walk in the Spirit, and you will not fulfill the lusts (desires) of the flesh." (Galatians 5:22) Note that he did not say, "Do the best you can", or "put these things into your life, and things will turn out right." It is only by walking in the Spirit that these qualities become part of our living.

Certainly, the fulfilled and happy person would be more likely to be the person walking in the Spirit. The final summation by Paul in this passage says, "against such there is no law," (verse 23b) speaking about the one walking in the Spirit.

DISCUSSION QUESTIONS

1. Can you name some ways that people use situation ethics in our society?
2. Why do you think it is important to have a specific standard of right and wrong?
3. What can a person do to encourage himself to walk in the Spirit?

CHAPTER TWO

LIVE WITH A VISION

King Solomon was the son of the greatest king Israel ever had. Solomon also was known as the wisest king and the wisest man to ever live. He wrote most of the Wisdom Books of the Old Testament.

Solomon had every reason to turn out wrong. He was born after the death of a baby that was born out of an adulterous relationship between his father and another man's wife. His father had her husband killed, trying to cover up the affair. His examples were not exemplary to say the least. His father was also a man of war. He was constantly fighting the Philistines or other nations, some over issues that were not worthy of battle.

There was a conversation between Jehovah and Solomon that changed Solomon's outlook, thus changing his life forever. God offered him riches, fame, or wisdom. He had to chose one. Solomon chose wisdom (which was a wise choice). Because God gave him wisdom, he also received fame and riches. In fact, he was the richest man on earth as well as the wisest.

That conversation with God became the source of Solomon's vision. Everything he did was for the sake of gaining knowledge (the collecting of facts and information) and the wisdom of using that knowledge. He passed that on to his children as he mentored them and his teachings were recorded by the scribes in his palace.

In those writings as recorded in Proverbs, Solomon said, "Where there is no vision, the people perish." (Proverbs 29:18 KJV) Leadership, success, living well, and motivation all fall by the wayside when people are without a vision. We do not see clearly on the roads of life when we have no vision of where we are going. We stumble in the darkness.

So it is with God. A person needs Him to teach him/her and build the spiritual life as well as to discipline the one who strays.

I know with God, as well as with my parents, I could trust them to put controls in my behavior that would mold me into a life that is useful. As I grow older, my experiences have shown this to be true. The rules my parents made or the parameters God set in my life, move behaviors into proper focus.

Most motivational speakers and leadership writers know about vision. They put it on paper and try to get leaders to find out where they are headed. They encourage leaders to turn those visions into goals and take people with them to reach those goals.

For most Christians, vision takes a different turn. They understand that a different viewpoint is taken:

First, people need a vision of who God is. Without a vision of His personality and place in our plans and lives, we simply drift around and cover the lack of vision by saying, "I just want to do His will." But that is a copout. We can have a vision of His will. If He guides us, we need to know we can trust Him.

To obtain a vision of God, we must read the descriptions of Him in the scriptures. The Psalms especially give a description of His presence and manner of working in people's lives. Some of those descriptions picture Him as:

Fortress (protection during trouble and battles)
Shepherd (leadership and care)
Buckler and Shield (protection from the evil enemy)
Rock (where one can stand; a foundation)
Shelter in the time of storm (obvious)
Provider (food, clothing, shelter, character, direction, etc)
Song (so rejoicing and satisfaction is shared)

The list goes on, but is obviously inexhaustible. God is everything for the Christian.

The vision is of sufficiency. God is sufficient for living, for succeeding, for living right and living well.

The vision also includes success and prosperity. (Prosperity will be described later in this book. It may not be what you think it is.)

A reading of Psalm 1 gives the Christian both a reason to rejoice, but also a motivation for living right in order to live well. Chapters following this one will be based on the formula presented in Psalm 1.

A vision is also needed of the enemy and how he works. Many Christians live in such a way, and think in such a way as to show blindness to Satan's influence and attacks on our thinking and living. But we don't have to be blinded to his devices. The New Testament says, "For we are not ignorant of his devices." (II Corinthians 2:11b NKJV)

For us to function well and succeed, we learn to know the devices he uses on us:

Deceitfulness -- he gives us partial truth and misconceptions to destroy our purity, love, and right living.

Lies -- if Satan can keep us from living right, he can keep us from living well. If he can get us to believe lies, he can keep us from living in truth and integrity.

False success and prosperity -- our definition of success and prosperity must not be based just on money. Some of the most successful people on earth are people who achieve their goals but are not rich in monetary measurements. Some of the most prosperous people have small bank accounts.

Misconceptions about others -- quick assumptions about people and their motives will cause much misunderstanding about what is happening to a person and what other people's motives are. Prejudice, misunderstandings, and bad relationships come from our misconceptions.

Satan attempts to cause those misconceptions by tempting us to make assumptions about others based on race and ethnicity, color of their hair (how many "blonde jokes" have you heard, or even told?), neighborhoods they live in, jobs they have, schools they attended, even denominations or churches they attend.

Just remember that "your adversary the devil as a roaring lion, walketh about, seeking whom he may devour." (James 5:8 KJV) He does not want any of us to live well. Especially, he does not want us to live right. He is our eternal enemy and wants to keep us from strong fellowship with our Father in Heaven.

God also wants us to have a true vision of our goals and have a dream of what we can become on earth. A person who has a vision actually has a dream. The main difference between a vision and a dream is that the one with a dream has an idea of what is possible. The person with a vision knows what can be achieved and how to get to the goal.

So many people have dreams. They wish for things to happen rather than making them happen. They hope something happens to get them from where they are to the realization of their dreams.

The person with vision knows the goals they expect to reach and even break those goals down into smaller goals. They map out their directions to the goals and follow those maps diligently. Hopes are realized when a person partners with God in faith and puts their own efforts and work into those steps. To many people work is simply a four-letter word. To others it is a lifestyle. A vision requires work in order to be reached.

As a youngster, I often ate Wheaties cereal. They used to put pictures of famous athletes on the boxes. Supposedly, those athletes ate their Wheaties for breakfast. The slogan was, "Wheaties, the breakfast of champions."

The first athlete to be featured on the face of the box was Bob Richards, olympic decathlon champion.

Bob Richards competed for the USA on three Olympic teams in the pole vault and decathlon and won AAU titles, including 17 in pole vault and 3 in decathlon. He also tied for the national collegiate title in those events as a student at the University of Illinois. Richards was the second man to pole vault 15 ft (4.57 m). He was the first athlete to appear on the front of Wheaties cereal boxes in 1958 (though not the first depicted on all parts of the packaging), and also was the first Wheaties spokesman, setting up the Wheaties Sports Federation, which encouraged participation in Olympic sports. Later, Richards was ordained as a minister in the Church of the Brethren. (From WIKIPEDIA)

As a child, Richards set a goal to become an olympic pole vaulter. It became his vision. He posted pictures of olympic vaulters everywhere he could, even on the ceiling above his bed. It was the first thing he saw every day, and became the thing he saw as he looked into his mirror or went into his room.

He arrived at a special place in life because he lived for that vision.

To live right, one must have a vision of living right and to honor God. "As he thinketh in his heart, so is he." (Proverbs 23:7a KJV)

Whatever a person's vision is, that will determine how that person lives.

To live right, one starts with a vision of right living. It will lead him to live well.

Part of living with a vision involves living with goals. I have a friend who is a manager in the Tupperware business. She is constantly talking about her goals and her vision of where she wants to be. She seeks God's purpose and will honor his leadership for her business. Often she shares those goals with my wife and me. She has us to pray for her to reach that vision and those goals. The biggest vision she has is driving up to her house and showing her family the brand new car she earns through her business.

She shared with me last week that the upper level leaders tell the managers that if their goal does not make them queasy in their stomachs, their goals are too small.

What are your goals and what is your vision?

DISCUSSION QUESTIONS

1. What can be added to the list of the attributes of our God?
2. What are some particular ways you have seen Satan work to harm the Christian?
3. How has God worked to counter those ways Satan tempts and opposes the believer?

CHAPTER THREE

LIVE IN LOVE

Throughout the Bible, we are told that God is love, and that He loves us with all His heart. It is the one truth that permeates every page and every story in the Scriptures.

We are created in the image of God (see Genesis 1 and 2). Since that is true, we must live lives of love because God IS love. (I John caps mine). Those of us who are believers in Christ, have experienced that love from God. John 3:16-17 tells us that "God so loved the world that He gave His only begotten son, that whosoever believeth in Him, should not perish, but have everlasting life. For God sent not His son into the world to condemn the world, but that the world through Him might be saved." (KJV)

If we have received the love of God through Jesus Christ, we must allow that love to flow *through* us as well as *into* us.

People today are starving for true, unconditional love. They are looking for it in all the wrong places. It cannot be found in drugs, in alcohol, in relationships that don't center on Christ, sex, porn, animals, or even within themselves.

Nothing but the love and grace of God can meet those needs deep within.

Every relationship and every person can know that love, but often we believers are the link that brings them into a personal relationship with the God who loves them so much that he offered up His only begotten son so that they could experience His eternal love.

As this is being written, we are suffering from shell shock in America because of the violence in various places. Hatred is being spread by different factions who wish to tear our dear country into shreds.

We have seen mass terror attacks against law enforcement, people of different ethnic backgrounds and about government decisions. Some incidents were random, some targeted innocent citizens walking on sidewalks.

One of the biggest issues before America at the moment is race relations. White supremacists and opponents of their positions waged an all out riot, attacking each other in Charlottesville, Virginia. A short time ago, several Dallas Police officers were shot while protecting citizens from being shot at a commercial business area. Some people are holding rallies on college and university campuses promoting prejudice and hatred in race relations.

It seems in today's society that if someone disagrees with us or belongs to a different ethnic group, race, denomination, religion, or speaks wrongly, we feel we have the right to kill them, terrorize them or injure them.

But we are wrong there.

We need to live in love, even for those who oppose us (maybe I should say, especially for those who oppose us).

A friend of mine serves as the leader of an organization

made up of a group of churches in a city that is known for violence and gangs who entangle people in drugs. Last year, he invited pastors and other leaders of the communities where he ministers to a monthly meeting of leaders of different doctrinal positions, races, or ethnicity, They share with one another the issues facing their communities and how they are approaching those issues with the gospel and with love. Few people know about it but, many doors of opportunity and ministry have opened because of it.

When I was a teenager, we took band trips in Trailways buses. Sooner or later, we would start singing the "silly" songs. One of those songs was *Love Makes the World Go 'Round.* During the 1960's era of music, many songs displayed those sentiments. But somehow, they lost their impact and value as time progressed. Today, we face so much hatred and bitterness toward one another. It naturally exhibits itself in the music that is most popular in the modern culture.

The person who lives right, knows the value of love Not only is there the knowledge of love's value, but there is a strong desire to love everyone. There is also an expression of that love through attitudes and actions. It involves respect, compassion, and works of helpfulness.

DISCUSSION QUESTIONS

1. What are some ways you have seen the love of God shown through someone loving someone else?
2. What actions can be taken to heal the brokenness of our society and culture that will display the love of God to broken people?
3. Is the church of Jesus Christ bringing healing to our generation of unbelievers? What can we do to improve the love relationship between the church and our community?

CHAPTER FOUR

LIVING RIGHT

Our children attended the school owned and operated by the church I pastored in Indiana. As Pastor, I was the School Administrator as well. One of the assignments we presented to the students each year was to memorize a portion of scripture that would stay with them throughout the school year and make their lives better in their adult years.

One year, we memorized Psalm 1. It is the very foundation of living right in order to live well. It says:

1. Blessed *is* the man
   Who walks not in the counsel of the ungodly,
   Nor stands in the path of sinners,
   Nor sits in the seat of the scornful;
2. But his delight *is* in the law of the Lord,
   And in His law he meditates day and night.
3. He shall be like a tree
   Planted by the rivers of water,
   That brings forth its fruit in its season,
   Whose leaf also shall not wither;

And whatever he does shall prosper.

4. The ungodly *are* not so,
   But *are* like the chaff which the wind drives away.
5. Therefore the ungodly shall not stand in the judgment,
   Nor sinners in the congregation of the righteous.
6. For the Lord knows the way of the righteous,
   But the way of the ungodly shall perish. (NKJV)

Let's take one portion of this Psalm at a time and explore what it says to us about our way of life.

The first section starts with a word that many people understand but maybe do not know the definition. The word is *blessed*. It means happy, satisfied, complete, and comfortable in your present state.

To be blessed, one must accept their circumstances as directed by God. He gives blessings, which means things he blesses people with. But to be blessed, it means one must be living with the blessing of God, that is, His encouragement and approval. Just as the custom of families in the Old Testament times, when the father was about to pass away, he would call the family together and formally pass on the blessing to the sons as his heirs, so God adds His blessing on to His children. It is as if He reaches out His hand and puts it on the person's head and pronounces His blessing on His child and imparts a blessing.

By doing so, He gives an inheritance, a portion of His kingdom, and all that goes with a father blessing his son.

The Bible says the Christians are "the children of God, and if children then heirs; if heirs, then heirs of God, and joint-heirs with Christ." (Romans 8:16b-17a KJV) In other words, believers inherit all that Jesus inherits from the Father.

The inheritance is twofold: first earthly or temporary; second, eternal or permanent. The earthly inheritance means His child gets God's prosperity in this life, which is temporary, materialistic, sometimes monetarily, temporal, or some other form of earthly blessings.

The permanent comes with the believer's state in eternity. It is also materialistic, it is not temporal, but is part of the heaven we inherit (eternal life) as children of God. (See John 1:12-13)

The next thing that is notable about Psalm 1 is, the blessed person is the one who keeps the right companions. The instruction is that the blessed person is the one who does not have the wrong people being the influence on a person.

As a former law enforcement chaplain, I have heard story after story of those who ended up in trouble because of the wrong companions who influenced their attitudes and behaviors.

One such story is about a young man in our church who was in a good career path, was married to a beautiful young lady, and was the father of two of the loveliest children you could ever meet.

His wife traveled out of state to have a visit with her parents. While she was away from home, the young man went to a neighbor's apartment (a female) and they began drinking beer. His companions that night were not good influences and kept giving more and more beer to the man.

Late in the evening, his companions left and he was alone with the young lady who lived there. He spent several hours alone with her, drinking more, and watching movies on television. It wasn't long until this married man made advances that the young woman spurned. Eventually, according to her accounts in court, he forced her to have sex and she accused him of rape.

I went to court with the young man and stood with him and his family as the judge pronounced him guilty and sentenced him to several years in prison. He was accompanied out of the courtroom by a representative of his employer where he was sent to the prison to serve his sentence. He lost his career, his family, and his future.

By seeking the wrong kinds of friends and allowing them to influence him, he lost everything.

I enjoy sitting in courtrooms. There I have seen judgment, wisdom, grace, and mercy. It gives me a great perspective into human nature.

One of the lessons I have learned from these visits, is that people often get in trouble because of the people who influence them and give them advice. I have seen many end up in prison or paying huge fines, even placed on probation for several years because of it.

Seeking advice from the right people. The first person to avoid is the advisor, counselor, or mentor who is ungodly or does not know God. The blessed person "walks not in the counsel of the ungodly." (Psalm 1: 1b NKJV) The reason is obvious: "If any of you lacks wisdom, let him ask of God, who giveth to all men liberally and upbraideth not." (James 1:5 KJV) Those who are in touch with God give better advice.

The natural, sinful mind does not know God, therefore cannot know the mind and heart of God. God's wisdom is usually counter to the secular, unredeemed mindset of the world.

If the person giving the advice is unsaved (ungodly), that person will not naturally seek the wisdom of God, but of man. The prophet Isaiah quoted God when He said, "For my thoughts are not your thoughts, neither are your ways my ways," saith the Lord." (Isaiah 55:8 KJV)

If a person desires a good and effective answer to any question dealing with lifestyles, decisions, or processes, that person should seek answers from the correct sources:

One of those sources is family. Solomon, the wise old man, when he wrote the book of Proverbs, encouraged his children to follow his wise advice.

The wisdom of God comes from several sources:

The Man of God (the Pastor or Bible Teacher or any person who walks with God)

The Word of God (the Bible)

T**he House of God** (the church, where that person should already be attending - Hebrews 10:25)

The People of God (totally committed Christians)

Any one of these could be wrong or give poor advice at one time or another. But, generally the person should seek the advice of all of these sources any time an important decision is made.'

One of my mentors as a young man advised a group of us to form a "cabinet". We were told to seek the advice of this cabinet anytime we needed the wisdom to make a strong and good decision. He reminded us that God's word says, "There is wisdom in the multitude of counselors."(Proverbs 11:14b)

The cabinet should include the following:

Our Pastor/Mentor - This is a man who walks with God and has the welfare of his flock on his heart.

A Christian Person in our career field - If we are

teachers, have a Christian teacher on our cabinet; if a person in ministry, have a ministry person on our cabinet (similar ministry is best); if an engineer, have an engineer; if a laborer, have a laborer, etc.

A person of great wisdom - a person who always seems to give the right advice to anyone. Proof is in the decisions people make after seeking their advice.

A person who is always looking out for our welfare - an encourager; a person who would tell us the truth even if it hurt our feelings.

A Christian whom we know walks with God - it is evident in their daily lives.

By asking the advice of each of these individuals, we would likely get the wisdom of God on any decision. They would share principles and even Scripture as we listen to their wisdom. They may not all agree. They confirm our thinking, they may open new avenues of thinking about our decisions.

We don't look for people who agree with everything we say or think. When we talk with them, it probably would not be wise to speak about how we feel about a decision. We do not look for confirmation, we look for wisdom.

When I was a young minister, I was serving churches as a Minister of Youth and Music. When I neared the age of thirty, I felt it was time to consider becoming a Pastor. As I received a call from a church and the search committee wanted to recommend to the church that I become their Pastor, I called the members of my cabinet. One married couple I had selected had been a real encouragement to me as I taught Sunday School in a large church as a layman. They were faithful people and seemed to look out for my welfare.

The question I presented was, "Do you think I could

pastor a church like this one?" I wanted to make sure others saw enough maturity and experience to properly lead the church.

Their reply was, "Sure, you can do anything you set your mind to."

I offered some follow-up questions and got the same answer. They offered no wisdom that was helpful. The next time I made an important decision, I skipped them on the phone calls.

Allow me to make some suggestions regarding the cabinet:

1. Alert them to the fact that you would like them to be on your cabinet and explain why you chose them and what you expect.
2. Don't wait for the "big moment" to call on them. Talk with them often (I suggest at least once a month). Let them know what is happening in your life.
3. You could also use them as an accountability group. If they have this wisdom, they also can help keep us out of "hot water." Honesty, openness, and trust are two way streets.
4. Pray for them. Love and respect are two-way streets.
5. Be available to them to contribute to their lives.
6. Honor them. Find ways to let them know how much they are appreciated and how valuable they are to your life.

DISCUSSION QUESTIONS

1. How have you been making major decisions? From whom have you sought wise counsel?
2. Who is on your cabinet, or if you have no cabinet, who would serve you well as cabinet members?
3. Is there a decision now in your life that such a cabinet would help in making the right decision?

CHAPTER FIVE

LIVE IN THE RIGHT CONVICTIONS

Notice that the Psalmist says that our position should be right. He shows us a progression when we seek advice from the wrong people.

The wrong counselors and mentors cause us to stumble if we walk in the counsel of the ungodly. When we walk in their counsel, we then stop walking and start to stand. If we stand, we tend to stand "in the way of sinners." Our lifestyle becomes one of inactivity and failing to move forward. When we were seeking advice, we were at least moving and trying to move forward.

When a person sits, that person becomes a complainer, whiner, and scorner. That is how people become "bullies" and live bitter lives. Life looks bleak because the progression has led to inactivity and lack of progress. When a person looks at a dead end life, other people's ideas and actions look bad and have no good purpose.

When we stand in the way of sinners, we are throwing in our lot with those who live ungodly and mostly unfruitful lives.

The book of Proverbs has much to say about that. (regarding throwing a young man's lot with angry and violent people.)

We become like those who surround us. Our friends and mentors are a great influence on our behavior, especially if we are listening to their voices.

We should surround ourselves with the kind of people we wish to become. If we desire to be successful, we should surround ourselves with successful people. If we desire to be financially stable, we should surround ourselves with financially stable people. If we desire to be strong leaders, influencing others in our lives, we should surround ourselves with strong impactful leaders.

The Tupperware Manager I mentioned earlier told me that the leadership people in the business told her and her fellow managers, "If you expect to be successful, surround yourself with successful people."

People tend to behave like those they "hang with." It is a given. The old saying is, "Birds of a feather flock together."

It is often difficult to live with good, strong convictions. By standing for convictions, especially if they are right and good, a person actually takes a stand for those things that govern the prosperous life.

Some people will automatically oppose you simply because your convictions contradict how they live and think. Don't let the opposition to your convictions stop you or change those convictions.

During the 1970's and 1980's, a good many pastors who were faithful to the Word of God and began Christian schools were arrested for things that they held as convictions in raising children and building strong families. They were jailed and compelled to stand trial for what the government officials were calling illegal and inferior schools. Eventually, the government was forced to release those pastors and church leaders and the schools were allowed to continue educating children with a biblical worldview. Their convictions were under fire and they stood to lose their right to exist; the pastors would serve long prison sentences; the sponsoring churches would be shut down.

One of the reasons the movement succeeded and the churches and schools won the battles was the Christians in those courtrooms took strong stands on their convictions. The attorneys would question those convictions and the reason they had to back off was the parents and churches learned the difference between convictions and preferences.

The courts held that a conviction is something a person would go to jail for or would die for. It is a hill on which one would die rather than change or give it up. A p is something one would strongly hold onto, but would not die for or go to jail before changing it.

Because the pastors, administrators, teachers, and parents held such deep and strongly held principles that were involved with the Christian viewpoint that they would go to prison or die for, the courts had no choice but to rule in their favor.

Whether one would agree with those convictions or not there would have to be a respect for the basis of their Christian viewpoints and beliefs. A deeply held belief must be the basis on which a Christian builds a life. Some of those deeply held beliefs must be convictions.

A person's character is shaped by the convictions that define that person. It will determine the moral fiber of a person. The integrity of a person is defined by those convictions.

Pick and choose acquaintances and friends well. They will mold and modify the convictions that define you. That is especially true of a person's mentors and advisors.

Standing in the way of sinners involves living the life the sinner lives. That means we follow their sinful patterns and commit the immoral, unholy, wicked acts that destroy a person's life and causes the impact of a person's life to be negative, even to the point of wickedness.

Violence, crime, and failure are the results that come from standing where sinners stand. To stand means to be stationary, without progress. That causes an unavoidable friction with the progress made by others. Progress always causes friction with anything stationary. A person becomes like a tire on a roadway. Friction is what causes the tire to wear out.

For three seasons, I served as a volunteer Chaplain for Arena Racing USA in Hampton Roads, Virginia. I noticed that on the track where there were turns, pieces of rubber gathered on the upper parts of the track which were banked at steep angles. I soon learned that the pieces of rubber came from the wheels of the race cars as they turned sharply at each of the four turns.

The cars were smaller versions of the NASCAR autos that race each Sunday during the spring and summer. But they ran over 50 miles per hour on a tenth of a mile track. The races were run during the winter months on an indoor track.

As they raced at a high speed for the small track, the wheels would meet resistance on the turns and even skid as they turned left. The rubber was left on the tracks so it would improve their grip on the track's high banked corners. My understanding is that this is also true for the full-size race cars.

Friction causes wear and tear and impedes progress in the same way in one's life.. Standing still is not an option. As life speeds by, progress will naturally cause friction to anything that is stationary.

Standing with sinners impedes successful and prosperous living and makes a negative impact on those who are walking with mentors and advisors who help the walk of the person traveling through life. Blessed is the person who does not stand in the way.

Sitting in the seat of the scornful usually involves criticism, mockery, and even bullying spiritually. People who are sitting are not moving forward unless they are riding a vehicle. In that case, they are actually not moving forward, but "going along with the ride."

Christians who are in that condition become critical of those who are busy serving Christ and His church. They seem to always have a better method of administration of the church, a better song to sing, a better sermon or lesson. The problem is, there is no involvement on their part that would prove them right.

I remember a church member who was constantly complaining and criticizing about the maintenance and construction of the buildings. The man always saw the shortcomings of our contractor when we remodeled part of the building.

In a meeting once, he fumed about the church buying toilet paper by the case so it was less expensive. The church had also grown and doubled the number of restrooms.

"I remember the last pastor brought a couple rolls of toilet paper from the parsonage when we needed it," he moaned. I informed him that would not be the case with me.

When he complained that the building committee and contractor were "doing it all wrong," one of the men asked, "how many buildings or remodels have you done?" That quieted him down quite a bit.

His attitude was typical of those who sit and become scornful.

Inactivity is not an option for the Christian, especially one who claims to love the Lord. God intends for His children to be active in ministry and outreach. If the child of God is active (walking and moving), there is little time for criticizing others.

Blessed is the man who does not sit in the seat of the scorner.

DISCUSSION QUESTIONS

1. Do people who are in the positions mentioned in Psalm One contribute to the progress of the local church? If not, what can be done to change their attitudes?
2. Do you agree with the definitions presented regarding the differences between a conviction and a preference? If not, how would you define them?
3. What happens to the spiritual life of one who is in one of the positions the Psalmist says to avoid? How would you describe that person?

CHAPTER SIX

THE TURNING POINT

I love the word when it appears in Scripture -- "BUT…."

That means it is in a different track than previously. It is a change of direction. Things change at this point. When the word appears in Psalm One, it changes from what the blessed man does not do, and changes to what the blessed person does do.

It is important that the person who wishes to be blessed of God needs to have a balanced life with strong do's and don'ts. That is what God is saying. Blessed is the person who does not line up with the wrong people and influences; blessed is the person who does other things right.

"His delight is in the law of the Lord." (Psalm 1:2 KJV). One of the biggest reasons a person is blessed by God is because he/she takes delight in God's law.

I often hear people, especially teens and young adults ask, "Why is God so strict?" or "Why doesn't God allow us to do what we enjoy? That is so unfair."

First of all, God doesn't make laws for the sake of hurting or pleasing people. The sins that harmed the human race after

Adam and Eve were cast out of the Garden of Eden are where God's concern is the strongest and He has the strongest statements about them.

For instance, He keeps sexual behavior limited to between a man and a woman and within the bounds of marriage.

Why does He do that when sex is so enjoyable and we have such a strong appetite for it?

Because it has the capability to produce a debilitating effect and can hurt people so deeply. It has dire consequences outside of marriage, or between people of the same sex. Diseases, emotional conflicts, and spiritual implications come when sexual sin takes place.

My wife and I counsel with people a great deal. Almost every person whom we have met with who was involved in sexual misbehavior, has had adjustment difficulties in marriage, especially when there were issues involving jealousy, regrets, unwanted pregnancies, abortions, and maladjustments in the intimate parts of their lives.

Every action has a result. A person who breaks one of God's laws suffers the result of breaking that law. Galatians 6:7 says, "Be not deceived, God is not mocked: whatsoever a man sows, that shall he also reap." (KJV) Conversely, when a person lives according to God's laws, there is a positive result. ("Whatsoever..." means it is true whether positively or negatively.) Either way, the person must accept the consequences of the actions.

But Psalm 1 is talking beyond the simple action equals consequences. It is talking about a person's lifestyle, a person's habits. "His delight is in the law of the Lord; and in His law doth he meditate day and night." His lifestyle is guided and motivated by the law of God.

A person's *delight* is that which makes that person happy, or satisfied. There is an inherent joy that causes the person to be absolutely giddy and fully satisfied in their inner being.

When a young lady is in love with a young man, nothing else really matters to her. She desires more than anything to be in his presence. She delights in him. When he feels the same way, the attention is mutual. Everything he does is important and enjoyable to her. If he is an athlete, she loves to watch him play, even if she has no interest in that sport at all. If he is a musician, she loves to hear him play, or to sing, even if she does not like the style of music he plays.

The same thing happens to a person whose delight is in the law of the Lord. Every part of God's word is something that is desirable and enjoyable. The person delights in His law. It is on the mind of that individual when they get out of bed in the morning, when they take a break at work or school, and when they go to bed at night.

In fact, this passage says the blessed person also meditates in the law of God (the Bible) "day and night."

The result of that kind of lifestyle is amazing. When a person spends so much time in the word of God, that person has a unique perception of life and how it should be lived. There is a knowledge of the wisdom and power of godly living. Not only that, the power of that knowledge shows itself in the thoughts and actions of the believer. It is a definite game changer.

No wonder that person is blessed!

I have known some people who love the Scriptures so much that they memorize as many verses as they can, One Pastor I met could quote the whole Bible and quoted portions of it verbatim during his sermons. Another man who taught evangelism in a Bible college had his students memorize scores of verses each semester. Personally, I have trouble with memorization, but I do try to memorize verses that are important to me.

The root of enthusiasm and passion in the life of the believer is a knowledge of God's word. What God loves, the believer reads about in the Word and falls in love with the same thing.

Also, the root of compassion and empathy in the life of the believer comes from the Spirit as the result of reading the Bible. Who can read the epistles of the New Testament without transferring the love and compassion found there into their own hearts.

A godly Pastor was preaching his sermon one Sunday and told of a man he knew who was prone to vent his anger on his family. When that happened, his house pet would cower and run away and hide. One evening, He trusted Christ as Savior and Lord. His anger left him and it was replaced with the love of Christ in him. His family noticed the difference and rejoiced. He told his Pastor, "My temperament has changed so much that even my dog sees the difference and greets me at the door every time I go home." John 3:16 and Romans 5:8 came alive as a result of God's salvation in his soul.

Delighting in the law of God produces a right relationship with the Father. It replaces the love of sin, lust, hatred, and bitterness. Mass shootings, terror attacks, rebellion, anarchy -- all of them filled with anger, frustration, and injustice.

I have several friends and acquaintances who serve and minister through their denominations. They go as quickly as possible to places across the country who are suffering and grieving due to loss of lives, property, and lifestyles. They continue to do so year after year. They return and tell how a couple thousand meals are served daily from a canteen trailer they took to the site of tragedies and weather-related incidents.

A layman I know who was once my chairman of deacons at our church is a semi-retired businessman. He is a volunteer chaplain at our local fire and rescue department.

Several times I have seen him at the scene of a fire or ambulance call in our neighborhood. He recently spent a week in Texas after the big hurricane that caused heavy flooding, loss of life, destroyed homes, and wreaking havoc with much of the state of Texas.

Why do those people give of their time and volunteer to be a person of trust and compassion? They are acting out of love for their neighbor and fellow man. It is the love of Christ living through them.

Delighting in the law of God produces a right relationship with family and other people. Families are restored. Enemies often become friends. Friendships grow deeper. We love people we once hated.

Recently, we have heard much in the news about tragedies, grief, anger, defeat, and disillusionment.

Delighting in the law of God produces a right set of principles for living. The Word of God contains a replaced value system where love and respect are the norms. The reason God blesses the person who delights in His law and meditates upon it, is that the laws contained in it become contained in our minds and hearts then produces actions.

A simple reading of the Bible, especially the New Testament, immediately shows the need for a person to love, even to love those who oppose us and become our enemies. It would do well if today's political discussions and those who produce the anger and terrorism in the streets of America would adopt the principles that Jesus Himself espoused in Luke 10:27 (KJV) 'And he answering said, Thou shalt love the Lord thy God with all thy heart, and with all thy soul, and with all thy strength, and with all thy mind; and thy neighbour as thyself."

That kind of love proves itself in how a person treats others in actions and words.

Delighting in the law of the Lord allows His love to flow through us out to other people. People need love, Everyone is looking for it. It is as if every person is wearing a sign hanging on a string or rope around the neck that says, "Love me, please."

This is played out in people who lose their mates in death or divorce. The missing lover has to be replaced by someone quickly, usually within eighteen months to two years. Many times the missing person is replaced without enough time to consider the consequences of marrying someone who is not suited to them or by someone who has little character or ability to establish a long-term relationship. This is especially true in marriages that have been filled with strong love and devotion to one another.

It is no wonder that Jesus emphasized that the first and greatest commandment is, Love God with all that is within you, and the second commandment is, Love your neighbor as yourself.

(By the way, if one looks closely at the Ten Commandments, you will find the first four commandments deal with loving God, and the rest of them are about our relationship with other people. The law of God is summed up by Jesus in the two commandments of love. By obeying these two commandments, people automatically follow the law of God as presented in Exodus chapter 20.)

When a person is delighting in the law of the Lord, that person allows the love produced from God's law to permeate life so fully that the overflow of that love reaches out to those who surround that person -- relatives, co-workers, neighbors, people on the street, homeless and needy people, and everyone who connects with the loving person.

Love automatically comes out of the obedience to Scripture. The Bible is an expression of the love of God. His law in which the prosperous person delights and meditates is how God has expressed His love to us. His commandments are there to protect His people from harm and establish strong loving relationships. So that love (remember -- God is love) first flows into the believer, then fills the person, and finally overflows onto others.

A friend who attended college at the same school at the same time I did, is an accomplished man who graduated from several schools with several degrees pastors a church in New England. Greater Glen Falls Bible Baptist Church in Hudson Falls, New York has been at his pastorate for 38 years. He has written several books, umpired baseball, served in the U S Air Force, has his pilot license and is a college professor. He has taught himself several languages, including Russian and has a great ministry. He recently posted the following on Facebook and I immediately asked him to allow me to include it in this book. He is gracious in every part of his life, including his marriage and family life. His life is prosperous by our definition.

He stated in the recent Facebook post that he could define his life as being "tough but simple." Simple because he allowed God's word to determine his choices and God to control outcomes. He acknowledged God's love and vowed to love Him in return. He said, "We get along very well. I need nothing less."

Thank you, Rev. Guy Goodell for your testimony of how Psalm 1 affects us.

DISCUSSION QUESTIONS

1. Can a person delight in Jesus and not delight in the "law of the Lord?"
2. How can we meditate on the law of the Lord day and night?
3. Draw a diagram that illustrate how the love of God works in you and through you.

CHAPTER SEVEN

SOLID FOUNDATION

Every action has a consequence. In Paul's epistle to the Galatians, he makes a strong statement of fact about the actions one performs. He said, "Whatsoever a man soweth, that shall he also reap." (Galatians 6:7 KJV)

Payday is coming. Someone may have already reaped the consequences of their actions. Maybe some haven't done so, and think there are no consequences in their situation. Be certain about this -- there are consequences for every action, some immediate, some delayed. But understand, payday *IS* coming.

Some paydays and consequences are bad, because the actions may have been bad, or at least questionable. A person has an auto accident and leaves the scene, the police eventually find that person and issue a summons, and probably a trial ensues. Payday!

A person lies. Over time, that lie may be questioned, or worse, it may be presented to the liar's face. A friend is lost; a family is divided; a business suffers because of it. Payday!

In the same token, good actions have consequences too.

Reaping the consequences of a good action may cause success, or promotion, or friendships, or some other pleasurable consequence. Payday!

One of my favorite television shows is *Shark Tank*. One of the interesting parts of the program are the extra things the "Sharks" do in certain situations. Of course it is a good action they take when they take a risk and support a new business. But often, the investor will extend kindness (like an eleven year old boy I saw once that one of the investors extended him a loan which he could pay off even the next year or whenever it would be convenient). Instead of just investing, there is advice, or some other action they put forth to help a person accomplish the goal and vision that is in the heart of the guest on the show. Smart investors know that kindness shown early in a person's life, will reap reward as well high regard from the entrepreneur that will have large benefits down the road.

Jonathan Edwards was a successful Puritan minister in Colonial days in the 1700's. He and his wife passed on to 11 children the values of a Godly life with truth and integrity. The family tree was traced from then for 150 years and the results of their living showed in their descendents at the turn of the twentieth century. Included in his descendents were 1 US Vice-president, 3 US Senators, 3 governors, 3 mayors, 13 college presidents, 30 judges, 65 professors, 100 lawyers, 80 public officials, and 100 missionaries.

Compare Max Jukes, who had 42 men from his bloodline in the New York prison system at the same period of time.

Whatever a person sows, that is what is reaped.

Verse 3 says, "And he shall **be like a tree planted by the rivers of water, that giveth forth his fruit in his season....**"

The tree planted by the water is going to have the advantage of water being constantly available.

Some plants like to be in direct sunlight. Some do not and they wilt and die if neglected and not given copious amounts of water. All plants flourish in the right amount of water.

We have a friend who helps with our lawn and landscaping. She gave us two potted "cobra" plants and said, "Don't leave these in direct sunlight. They need some light, but they do not do well in direct sunlight."

We left the plants at the front of the house under the picture window. Soon, the afternoon sun in the west beat down on those plants. They began to get some brown edges on the large leaves. I had to spend about a half hour trimming back those leaves that had been affected and removing those that had died.

I moved the plants out of the direct afternoon sun and saw that they received plenty of water every day. Soon the plants were flourishing, producing new leaves and blooming the white cobra-like "flowers" in plentiful amounts.

The Lord says, that when we delight in His word and meditate on it, we produce fruit like a plant that is planted near a river. It draws the moisture from the soil on the river bank and flourishes and gives forth fruit for human pleasure. A tree that is planted by a stream of water draws moisture from the stream. It becomes strong and healthy. Those are the trees that people swing with a rope into the water and enjoy the days of summer.

Where are you planted? Is your life fruitful? What kind of fruit do you produce? Is it ripe and healthy and strong?

If not, inspection is needed. Answering the difficult

questions become necessary, weeding out the sins and behavior that harm the way to flourishing.

Sin takes many forms; some of which we tend to overlook and consider more of a "bad habit" or inconsequential. A flourishing life must have constant pruning and removing of deadness and blight To live a life that does not have our best attention and effort is sinful because it keeps one from doing what glorifies God. Colossians 3:17 says, "And whatsoever ye do in word or deed, do all in the name of the Lord Jesus, giving thanks to God and the Father by him." (KJV) Doing all in the name of the Lord brings glory to HIm.

Sin always robs a person of God's personal best blessedness of that person. Keeping the life delighting in the law of the Lord and meditating in it day and night causes the kind of behavior that God can and will bless.

The secret to delighting in God's law is to "meditate in it day and night."

Meditation is something few Christians consider. It has fallen into disfavor among Biblical believers because of the "transcendental meditation" practices of Eastern religions and New Age practices of meditating. But one must not allow the abuses of meditation to hinder our path to "blessedness."

It is interesting to note that God blesses those who practice biblical meditation.

Meditation's synonyms include contemplating the word of God, spending time thinking deeply about His word. It usually means we have to not only read it, but study it. Much can be said about a person delving into the application as well as the translation of biblical truth. We should ask, "What is the human writer saying in this passage?" and, "How does that apply to my life?"

Other synonyms include, musing, pondering, consideration, reflection, or deliberation. These words should probably involve much prayer and concentration on biblical passages.

The reading and meditation of the Psalms is particularly helpful in worship. Those wonderful passages lead us to heavenly places in our thinking, therefore in our actions daily. Meditating on the songs of David and the main musicians of his kingdom will teach us how to worship the Holy God of Heaven and earth -- the Creator of the universe. The Psalms will lift our hearts and souls to His presence when a person fixes the mind on them.

The meditation of the book of Proverbs will lead one to understand the wisdom needed to face decisions and function in an orderly society.

The meditation on Song of Solomon (Canticles) will help people to express marital love and bring bliss and happiness to the love life at home.

Meditating on the Epistles of the New Testament will help one to treat other people with dignity and respect. Behavior toward neighbors, friends, coworkers, and family will be greatly enriched by those musings.

No wonder the Psalmist proclaims that life will be blessed, happy, and joyful. Meditating on God's law of love and purity will touch every part of an individual's being.

Living right through the law of the Lord will enrich every person who chooses to meditate on His law day and night.

Living right by meditating in God's law day and night will result in living well.

The Apostle Paul certainly found this true. He talked about "walking in the Spirit." In that vein, he wrote to the church in Galatia about the "fruit of the Spirit." He said, "The fruit of the Spirit is love, joy, peace, longsuffering (patience is the translation by some), gentleness, goodness, faith, meekness, temperance. Against such there is no law...." (Galatians 5:22-23 KJV) It is a simple assumption that if one wishes to walk in the Spirit, there must be an understanding of the message of the Spirit of God who gave the "God breathed" word. Paul assumed such a life would be the result of being in such communion with the word of God.

Everyone should consider the result of the presence of the Holy Spirit in a Christian's life. Such a life produces love, joy, and the rest of the fruit just mentioned. It is the kind of life that has no law forbidding it to live that way.

In the first Psalm, the promise is that a person who meditates in the law of the Lord day and night, will live the blessed life everyone longs for.

DISCUSSION QUESTIONS

1. Have twenty-first century believers lost the ability to meditate? What contributes to the ability or lack of it?
2. Does God's forgiveness always remove the consequences of a believer's sins?
3. What warnings would you give to young adults about their behaviors?

CHAPTER EIGHT

HAVE YOUR CAKE AND EAT IT TOO

When a person desires to keep something and at the same time, give it away or let someone else have it too, or one wishes to have the good and bad consequences of their behaviors and attitudes at the same time, they are said to "Want their cake and eat it too." The common wisdom is that you can't have it both ways.

But the Psalmist did not seem to grasp the concept. He believed one could live right and at the same time, live well. Note his words -- "...Whatsoever he doeth shall prosper."

If a man or woman does not fraternize with the ungodly, but delights in the law of the Lord, meditating in it day and night, whatever that person does prospers. Is that correct?

It certainly is promised by God through David, the Psalmist. He also said a similar thing to Joshua when he took over the leadership of the Israelites after the death of Moses. In Joshua 1:8-9 He says, "This book of the law shall not depart out of thy mouth; but thou shalt meditate therein day and night; and thou shalt observe to do all that is written therein: for then thou shalt make thy way prosperous, and then thou shalt have good success." (KJV)

To be prosperous, by definition, is to be successful in material terms or to flourish financially. Does this mean then that those who believe in the "prosperity theology" of our day are right? They say that God does not want anyone to do without material blessing. Some even say that if one has God's approval, He will heap money, health, and happiness on that person.

Those who oppose such theology attempt to disprove such thinking. The Christian life is one of sacrifice and doing without such prosperity and is their mantra.

I remember interviewing and preaching a trial sermon for a church in a famous university town. The area of the country was enticing and the church was one of fellowship and evangelistic ministry. It was quite inviting. During the interview with the search committee and leadership of the church, I kept hearing a theme that did more to define the church to me than the information that was supplied by the committee.

"We don't have any politicians, bankers or company CEO's in our church," they kept saying. After hearing it several times, I realized they were limiting their ministry to the working middle class and saw it as a badge of spirituality that they did not seek nor serve those who were in the upper sphere of the financial world.

So, have we missed out on the message and will of God? Do we do without because we don't believe the promises of God. After all, there are over 3,000 promises from Him in the Bible. It is just a matter of believing -- right? What gives?

First of all, what has been misunderstood is not His promises, but His definition of prosperity, and the path to prosperity. Let's take a look.

A key phrase in the passage we are exploring is "whatsoever he doeth shall prosper." In defining God's idea of prosperity, it must be understood that He thinks in terms of the complete person. The world's concept is single focused. Their concept is that the only measure of prosperity is financial and materialistic. The measure of prosperity is how much one has in the bank or invested and how many things a person possesses.

In other words, the one with the most toys wins.

Sadly, such thinking has entered into the discussion and thought about eternity. Being that kind of prosperous may suit this life well, but is disastrous in eternal matters. It neither guarantees Heaven nor one's standing in eternity. Even if the financially prosperous person is saved or if there is a sharing of the increase with those less fortunate, it does not offer eternal life in Heaven nor give eternal rewards.

Money does not move God. What moves God is faith, prayer, faithfulness, and righteousness. In fact, Jesus warned against the enticement of riches. He said that a rich man had a tough time getting into Heaven.

God's idea of prosperity is one of the complete person. When a person follows all the steps as described in Psalm 1, God blesses those principles and sends prosperity in all aspects of the person's life. That would include any efforts the person undertakes: career, worship, family relationships, hobbies, education, income, any efforts put forth by the individual.

It does not necessarily mean a person becomes rich, but it does mean a person will do things that "flourish" (a synonym for prosper).

God's opportunity for people is to ***LIVE RIGHT TO LIVE WELL.***

The concept is intensified when one reads verses 4 and 5.

DISCUSSION QUESTIONS

1. Why do you think it is hard for a rich person to get into Heaven? Is that God's doing or man's?
2. Does the concept of "whatsoever he does shall prosper" include financial prosperity or exclude it?
3. Name some ways God prospers a person who follows the "Live Right" formula and explain how the person lives well.

CHAPTER NINE

SORRY GUYS

"But the ungodly are not so: but are like the chaff which the wind driveth away. Therefore, the ungodly shall not stand in the judgment, nor sinners in the congregation of the righteous." (Psalm 1:4-5 KJV)

That is pretty definitive! God differentiates between the righteous person and the unrighteous (ungodly) person. It is also obvious that the person God does not put His hand of blessing on walks in the counsel of the ungodly, stands in the way of sinners, sits in the seat of the scornful, His delight is not in the law of God, much less meditated upon at all.

And love is not part of the equation. Winning is not the most important thing; it is the only thing.

The usual attitude of the ungodly is "get more any way you can. If you have to step on others to climb the ladder of success, so what?"

Honesty, integrity, truth, purity, and other Godly character traits are not the most important parts of the life of the ungodly.

The congregation of the godly is made up of Christians

who love the Word of God and try to live it. Their direction in life is governed by its principles. Decisions are governed by those same principles. Those directions and decisions are in complete conflict with the ungodly.

Though everyone has to face the judgment of society and popular opinion, that is not the most important judgment that is faced. It is not the final say about the issue of success and prosperity.

The most important judgment is facing God with the thoughts and intents of the heart. That is the judgment which requires living right and determines if a person lives well.

A strong consideration here is that the judgment of God is not something that is an event down the road after death or the end of time. It is an ongoing process and daily prosperity and flourishing depends on God giving favorable judgments on the thinking and living and the principles governing that life.

The story is told of a contractor who built houses and developed communities of homes. He had a son who had grown up and matured in the environment of his father's business. As he matured into adulthood, he came to the realization that he wanted to follow in his father's footsteps.

The son had dated the same young lady from the time they graduated from high school. They were engaged and soon to be married. The time of the wedding was drawing near.

The son walked into his dad's office and said, "Dad, I have really enjoyed working with you these last several years. Now that I am getting married, I think I am ready to take over part of the business and be equal partners with you."

"I agree," said the father. "I just bought a nice piece of

property and you have the responsibility to build the house that will sit on that property. Here are the plans for the house. Build it to the dimensions in the blueprints. You will choose all the materials and the specs. Choose them well. I will not supervise you or even check up on your progress. If you need advice or help, I am available, but all the decisions will be made by you. Remember all I have taught you."

The young man was ecstatic. He would put all his knowledge to work and his training would guide him as he built the first house of his management career.

The house was elaborate in its design and had several bedrooms and a den and all the amenities, such as a swimming pool and tennis court. As he built, decisions were made about the quality and spending for materials and workmanship. He knew that a final accounting and profitability would be made by his father and by the inspectors for the city. He was extremely frugal as he had been taught by his father. However, he often bought inferior quality materials for plumbing, electrical, and other parts of the house. "These things are hidden and no one will know for about five years that any of the materials and workmanship are inferior," he thought.

The day the house was completed was just days before the wedding. He and his wife had planned to move into an apartment until they could afford to build their own home, which would probably be a couple years down the road.

The son proudly presented his father with the keys to the home along with the deed and paperwork, showing the project coming in below budget, leaving room for a good profit at sale.

The father returned the keys and paperwork to the son

and said, "Son, you were building this house for you and your bride to live in. This is your wedding gift."

Imagine the son's amazement and the private guilt and subsequent embarrassment of explaining to his bride why some of the problems came in the coming months and years.

People are constantly facing the reality of how they build their lives on principles that will hinder their ability to flourish and prosper. Yet, daily, the quality of living and character are being judged, not by the court of public opinion, but by God himself -- the perfect, all knowing judge of the universe.

And He said, "The ungodly...are like the chaff, which the wind driveth away." (Psalm 1:4 KJV) In other words, they do not flourish and prosper.

God expects people to live right in order to live well. Following the principles of living right produces a prosperous way of life.

The concluding verses say, "For the Lord knoweth the way of the righteous; but the way of the ungodly shall perish."

The Judge has spoken.

DISCUSSION QUESTIONS

1. What are some of the ways that the "harvest" comes to the ungodly?
2. If a person has not been living right, how can the change be made to live right instead?
3. Are you **Living Right?**

CHAPTER TEN

THE REST OF THE STORY

There is something I have noticed about those who are living the prosperous life as described in the Bible and this book. It makes the prosperous life more fun and more exciting as we see God work through us.

Some people call it "paying it forward." Others call it "living the life of generosity." Both Jesus and the Apostle Paul talked about it. It is a vital part of the prosperous life. The enjoyment comes when you see others enjoy the prosperity you share.

The churches of Macedonia experienced that when the Apostle Paul requested their financial help in helping the believers that were being persecuted and shut out of the benefits of society. The amazing thing about that is the circumstances they were in at the time. Paul described the Macedonian churches as living in "great trials and afflictions." They also were living in "deep poverty." (Read II Corinthians 8:1-7)

The story gets even better. The churches gave in spite of their conditions. Paul said that they even "gave beyond themselves." It leaves the impression that they gave beyond what one would expect even from someone in normal conditions.

That is true generosity!

EXAMPLES OF RECENT HISTORY:

In our modern society, there are prosperous people who are also generous. Some of them are well-known. For instance, the Cathey family (owners of Chick Fil A) is famous not only for their standing on the convictions of being closed on Sunday, the Lord's Day, but also for their generous support of their young employees by giving scholarships to those who have worked for a certain length of time for their company. They have franchisees who have fed thousands of families and workers during natural disasters and tragic circumstances.

The Twentieth Century was one of the most prosperous times in history. After World War Two, the Baby Boomers brought some of the most advanced improvements in the meaning of prosperity and especially economically. Remarkably, many people were recognized for their generosity. There was a connection between their success and their generosity. (Understand that they were not only generous because of their success but were generous before they were successful. In fact, their personal generosity contributed to their growth and prosperity.)

One of those men was R. G. LeTourneau. He was an avid inventor, mostly of giant earth moving equipment. Approximately 70 percent of the earth moving machinery and engineering vehicles used by the Allied Forces during World War II were the results of his work. Using rubber tires on such vehicles was one of his innovations, including using the low-pressure, heavy duty tires.

Toward the end of his life, LeTourneau was contributing approximately ninety percent of his income to charities and Christian causes, including founding the university named after him and his wife, Evelyn. LeTourneau University has primarily been a training ground for technical missionaries and engineers along with aeronautical sciences.

Another example is James Cash Penney, a retail businessman who developed a chain of retail stores that has grown to over 1,000 stores. He emphasized customer service, fair prices, good value, and a generous return policy. Main Street America in the Twentieth Century nearly always included the JC Penney Department Store. Mr. Penney was a generous man who paid his employees fairly, and often helped the poor and supported many causes and business people who had lost their jobs and career setbacks. The Penney Family Fund endows organizations in several states that work to advance human rights, community social, political, economic empowerment, government accountability and environmental sustainability according to Wikipedia. The fund carries on the legacy of J C Penney.

BENEFITS OF GENEROUS LIVING:

THE BLESSING OF GOD. Our Lord adds His blessing to the life and careers of those who live generously. There are many examples of that being so. In Genesis 14, Abraham gave Melchizedek ten percent of all his possessions. In Genesis 28 Jacob followed his grandfather's example and gave ten percent of his possessions to God. King David said, "I will not offer to God that which costs me nothing." (See 2 Samuel 24:24 and surrounding verses)

The Old Testament has many references of men who were generous, including Solomon, Malachi, the prophets and others. In the New Testament, we see the generosity of the Good Samaritan who took care of the expenses above and beyond the medical help to the victim of thieves. Paul commended the churches who supported other churches and the needy in cities where he had ministered.

Jesus spoke more about giving than he did about most subjects. In fact, He said to give over 1,000 times.. It is obvious that God desires for us to be generous.

In thinking about generosity, I came up with an acrostic:

Give, Give, Give
Every time you have occasion
Never be selfish
Enjoy sharing with others
Remember God loves you and shares with you
Owe no man nothing
Unleash your love
Share the bounty

JOY OF HELPING THOSE WHO CANNOT HELP THEMSELVES.

I recently saw a sign quoting John Bunyan as saying, "You have not lived today until you have done something for someone who cannot repay you."

Many people today cannot fend for themselves. Unfortunately, the American church has delegated the care of such people to the government or other non-profit entities.

We have become calloused to the suffering of those outside our church's congregations. We tend to overanalyze and offer criticism about their lifestyles. The life of generosity is one that jumps into action when it encounters the homeless, helpless, or the harmed. Where there is a need, generosity and compassion gravitate to the point of need and tries to meet that need, even at great cost to the one who is the giver.

The person who is living right will live well by living the life of generosity.

DISCUSSION QUESTIONS

1. What is the greatest gift of generosity that you have seen from someone other than God's gift of salvation through Christ?
2. Do you think the life of generosity is the result of the prosperous life, or is it part of Living Well?
3. Who is the most generous person you have ever met? Are they living right, living well, or both?

Printed in the United States
By Bookmasters